EXPLORERS WANTED!
In the Wilderness
Simon Chapman

Simon Chapman
EXPLORERS
WANTED!

In the Wilderness

LITTLE, BROWN AND COMPANY

New York ❧ Boston

Little, Brown and Company

Time Warner Book Group
1271 Avenue of the Americas, New York, NY 10020
Visit our Web site at www.lb-kids.com

First U.S. Edition: June 2005

First published in Great Britain by Egmont Books Limited in 2003
ISBN: 0-316-15542-X
10 9 8 7 6 5 4 3 2 1
COM-MO
Printed in the United States of America

CONTENTS

SO...YOU WANT TO BE A WILDERNESS EXPLORER?

Do you want to...
Brave the great **Siberian wilderness**...?

Canoe **raging rapids** on **wild white water**...?

Avoid being eaten by **bears, wolves, and wolverines**...?
If the answer to any of these questions is **YES**,
then this is the book for you. Read on...

THIS BOOK GIVES you the lowdown on exploring the Siberian taiga forests, an environment of climate extremes stacked with potentially lethal wildlife. You'll learn what you need to take and how to deal with the hazards, and you'll find out about some of the people who tried to explore there before you.

YOUR MISSION ...

should you choose to accept it, is to lead an expedition into the heart of the Siberian wilderness in search of a giant meteorite crater.

June 30, 1908, Tunguska, Eastern Siberia. A lump of rock from outer space, the size of a tennis court, zoomed into Earth's atmosphere and exploded mid-air above the Siberian taiga, like an atom bomb going off. Trees were knocked flat for miles around and the noise of the explosion could be heard hundreds of kilometers away. But what happened to the meteorite? Did it entirely vaporize on contact with Earth or did it smack into the ground, creating an enormous crater? Recently, a light plane heading to an oil-drilling station near the River Gorbushka reported strange things.

The pilot had lost his way in a bank of low cloud. When he dipped his plane to get a better view of the ground he didn't recognize what he saw. What's more, his compass needle kept swinging crazily. It simply would not point North. Looping around, the pilot spotted a circular, bowl-like area among the forested hills.
A meteorite impact crater?

Now you've decided to go there, to locate the impact site and perhaps even find a piece of the meteorite that you believe caused it.

Time to set the scene ...

Let's find out some vital facts about Siberia and its environment before the mission gets underway.

The taiga is a vast coniferous forest, stretching from Finland all the way across the Eurasian continent to the Pacific Ocean. The forest is even bigger than the Amazon rainforest in South America, and nearly all of it lies within just one country — Russia. This is the great Siberian wilderness.

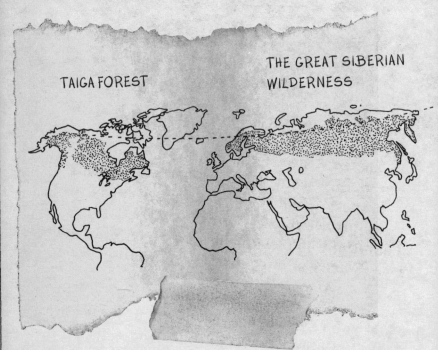

TAIGA FOREST

THE GREAT SIBERIAN WILDERNESS

Across the Pacific, the forest carries on through Alaska and Canada. Many of the creatures found there are the same, though they may have different names.

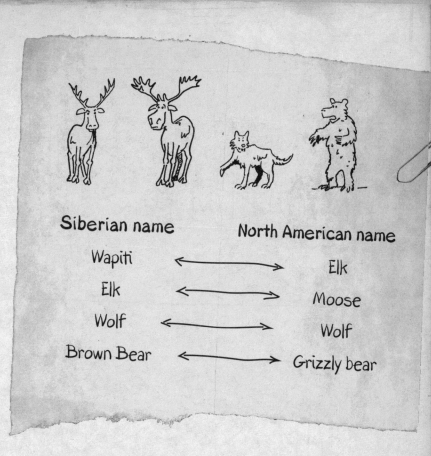

Siberian name		North American name
Wapiti	⟷	Elk
Elk	⟷	Moose
Wolf	⟷	Wolf
Brown Bear	⟷	Grizzly bear

So what is the Siberian wilderness like? This depends on what time of year it is. The big thing to understand is that the climate has two very different characters.

A short, hot, insect-ridden summer and a freezing, snowbound winter. Some parts of Eastern Siberia have the largest temperature range of anywhere in the world; from a positively tropical 38°C in June and July down to a chilly -68°C in the cold, dark winter. Brrr!

WINTER

SUMMER

So close to the Arctic, days are short in the winter. By December it's dark (dim even at midday), bitingly cold, and, unless you know where to look or are prepared to dig through the snow, there is no food to gather. There are hardly any animals around either—many of them have either found a sheltered place to hibernate, or have moved away until the weather gets warmer.

But ... summertime and the living is easy, right? Well, no. It can snow even at this time of year. It can be fine all morning then there'll be a blizzard by lunchtime. This will make it extra difficult to choose what supplies to take with you on your mission.

You've decided to set off in the summer — the best time for an expedition. The rivers are high and fast-flowing with the snow that melted in the spring, and all the plants are growing at full speed in the few months before the cold weather returns. Bright green new needle leaves have grown on the larches and birches, and the air is warm, humid, and buzzing with insects.

But away from the sunlit glades, the trees are tightly packed and it's gloomy and dim ...

The forest floor is covered in moss and fuzzy lichens and, occasionally, ferns grow among the fallen branches and pine needles. Pushing your way forward, you're up against more trunks, more moss, more of the same. It's clear you're going to need some sort of plan to navigate your way through this endless forest or else you're going to get yourself very lost.

Suddenly . . . you hear something.
You spin around. What could it be?

A bear?
One swipe from its paw would knock you flat. Then you're easy meat.

A ravenous wolf?
And where there's one, there's usually a whole pack.

An elk?
You won't want to tangle with antlers like these when the bull's blood is up in mating season.

Perhaps a wolverine?

It probably wouldn't attack you while you were upright and healthy, but what if you injured yourself?

Or is it just a dead branch, dislodged by the wind, tumbling down to Earth?

Looking up, you can see the treetops swaying. No more strange noises, so perhaps you're OK for now. But clouds have blown across the sun and already you can feel the temperature dropping. The mosquitoes and deer ticks are biting. The weather seems to be turning. Do you have enough food and cold-weather gear? Do you have the equipment to improvise from the resources you find around you?

Are you properly equipped?

Chapter 1
GETTING READY

THESE ARE YOUR basic survival needs:

FOOD   FIRE   SHELTER   WATER

You will have to be ready for every possibility. Most likely it'll be reasonably warm, but there could be rain ... and even this late in the year, snow. Below are the clothes you'll be wearing and the equipment you'll take.... Remember, you don't need to wear all of this gear all of the time.

STURDY BOOTS

LONG UNDERWEAR

FLEECE TOP

LIGHT PANTS

HAT

SOCKS

BREATHABLE OVER-JACKET, OVER-PANTS

SPARE, DRY CLOTHES IN BACKPACK

FIRE-LIGHTING STUFF: LIGHTER, MATCHES, FLINT, AND STEEL

LOCK-KNIFE, HATCHET, CORD

MEDICAL KIT

WASH KIT

FLASHLIGHT, PLENTY OF BATTERIES

TENT

SLEEPING BAG

ROLL MAT

COOKING GEAR

 FOOD — light stuff like pasta, dried meals; some cans, but only for the start . . . chocolate or other **morale** food to keep your spirits up when you are feeling cold, wet, and miserable . . .

 MAPS (if available)

 GPS (You might want to consider taking one of these. It uses satellite signals to tell you your exact position anywhere on the planet . . . only really useful if you have a good map.)

COMPASS

RUSSIAN PHRASE BOOK
Postcards or pictures of home to show people you meet, and some small presents for them.

And if you can afford to carry the extra weight, how about taking a CAMERA and some BINOCULARS to view the wildlife?

Also, how about hiring a guide? You could benefit from an expert tracker who can find a way through the wilderness, forage food from the land, and keep you out of trouble with bears and wolves. You've heard of a guy called Sergei. A friend of a friend recommended him. . . . When you meet Sergei, he tells you he's got Evenk tribal blood in his family and that his uncle, Vlad, lives in the taiga beyond the Gorbushka river. Sergei has lived all his life in cities, but the "ways of the wilderness," he assures you, will come back to him once he gets into the taiga.

In your bag there are some key basic items, from which you can make do or improvise for the four **survival needs**. Most vital is a good knife. You can use it to help build **SHELTER**, hunt, and prepare **FOOD**, hollow out a container to hold **WATER**, or even strike a flint stone on it to make **FIRE**.

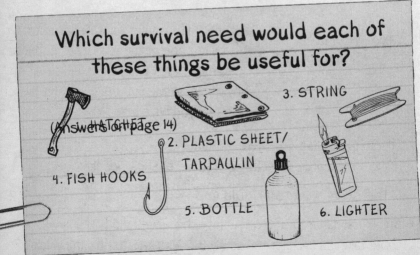

Which survival need would each of these things be useful for?

(Answers on page 14)

1. HATCHET

2. PLASTIC SHEET/ TARPAULIN

3. STRING

4. FISH HOOKS

5. BOTTLE

6. LIGHTER

But what do you do if you don't have the key basic items? Think about it. Many of the people who lived in the area up until fairly recently, tribes like the Tungus, would have had to make do with what they could find in the forest. Here's how:

1. HATCHET
   (flintstone axe)

2. PLASTIC SHEET/TARPAULIN
   (deer hides)

3. STRING
   (animal tendons, strips of certain tree barks)

4. FISH HOOKS
   (hooks made from bones or thorns)

5. BOTTLE
   (animal skin or bladder water bag)

6. LIGHTER
   (fire-starting bow)

If you lost your equipment and you had the time and the skills, you too could improvise.

ANSWERS from page 12

ANSWERS from page 12

1. Shelter
2. Shelter or collecting water
3. Shelter or food (fishing lines or making animal traps)
4. Food
5. Water
6. Fire

So, you've now got your gear together — and there's a lot to take, isn't there? You might just about be able to carry all that on flat, level ground, but you're about to lug it through some of the hardest terrain on the planet. You will want some sort of transportation, for part of the time at least. But it's not that easy....

This is the size of the problem . . .

- There are no roads, except a few logging tracks around the southern edges.
- The coniferous forest cover is very dense — little fodder there for pack animals, or food for human porters.
- You'll have to cross swampy lowlands with lakes and rivers, and steep, rocky highlands.
- You'll face some sudden changes in weather conditions.

The Options

A. Set out on foot with human porters (who, incidentally, will have all their own gear to carry too).

B. Take pack horses.

C. Hire a motor vehicle.

D. Charter a boat.

YOUR ROUTE

This is a sketch map of the terrain ahead of you drawn by the pilot who saw the crater. Now it's up to you to decide what to do.

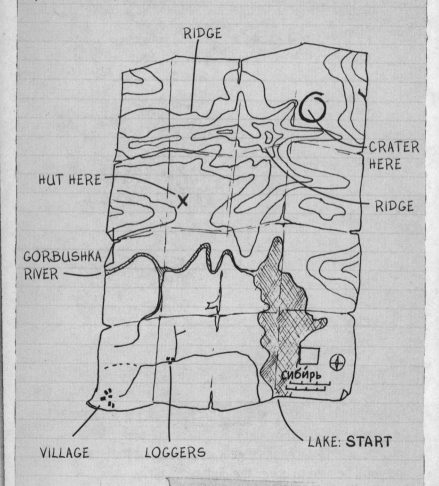

RIDGE

CRATER HERE

HUT HERE

RIDGE

GORBUSHKA RIVER

СИБИРЬ

VILLAGE   LOGGERS   LAKE: **START**

1. Which transportation option is not available to you?
   A, B, C or D?

2. Which option will you need for the lake and the river?

3. What sort of vehicle could you hire at the logging camp that could take your answer to question 2?

   E. A logging truck?
   F. A bulldozer?
   G. A four-wheel-drive jeep?

(Answers on page 18)

As you can see from the map, the taiga in that region is a mass of shallow lakes, marshes, and forests. You decide to follow the course of several joined ribbon lakes and canoe the outflow stream. Following the river may take you and Sergei slightly out of your way, but you've opted for this route, as you'll be able to carry more gear in the boat at the start . . . and you'll be able to cover the distance fast.

To get to the lake you decide to hitch a ride on a logging truck. The Siberian taiga — like other forests across the world — is being cut down fast to make everything from furniture to plywood doors and even paper. You see convoys of trucks taking tree trunks to sawmills. And there are empty trucks coming back the other way. Sergei reckons that it shouldn't be too difficult to find one that will take you and the five-meter canoe he's borrowed to the edge of the lake.

ANSWERS from page 17

1. B No pack horses
2. D
3. E

Chapter 2
LAKES AND MOUNTAINS

CANOEING. IT'S EARLY morning. The air is still, crisp and cold. Mist rises over the clumps of reeds and long grasses at the water's edges. Ahead of you, hazy in the distance, is the rugged range of hills that is your goal.

All is quiet. You are aware of the faint splash of your paddles dipping in the water and the plaintive cry of a great northern diver.

There are some ducks on the water, diving under from time to time to resurface some distance away. The ducks keep well clear of the  canoe. They are not unlike ducks you might see in a park at home, but these ducks are wild and too used to being hunted to come within rifle range of you.

Tiny biting flies, midges, are already out in force. Clouds of them hover around the lake's edges, so it makes sense to stay out in the middle of the lake and keep paddling; the flies can't move that fast. If you don't, any uncovered skin will soon be dotted with little, raised bumps and the itching will drive you crazy over the days to come. Before this expedition, you'd have thought that the tropical rainforest was the worst place for biting bugs. Even if it is, the Siberian wilderness must come a close second for sheer insect unpleasantness.

And it's not just midges; once you enter the trees you'll also have to contend with a mob of mosquitoes, horseflies and ticks — all out for a sip of your tasty blood. Mmm!

20

So, what can you do to prevent yourself from being bitten?

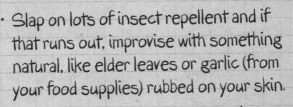

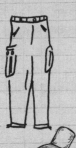

- Cover up. Wear long pants and a long-sleeved shirt.

- Wear a head net when the bugs are really bad.

- Slap on lots of insect repellent and if that runs out, improvise with something natural, like elder leaves or garlic (from your food supplies) rubbed on your skin.

- When you set up camp, put some damp leaves over the fire to make smoke. This will keep the midges away.

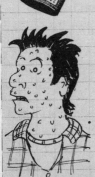

- Or, just learn to suffer the bites.

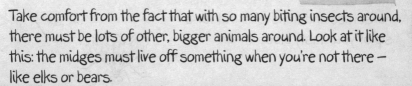

Take comfort from the fact that with so many biting insects around, there must be lots of other, bigger animals around. Look at it like this: the midges must live off something when you're not there — like elks or bears.

Also, what about all the fly-catchers, swallows, and dragonflies that eat small flies? Wouldn't the taiga be dull and depressing to visit without the wildlife to appreciate? Of course, you may not feel like this when your body is a mass of itching bites that stop you sleeping and you have masses of ticks to pry off.

Today, you're insect-free once you're away from the lakeside. There's enough of a breeze to blow away any midges, though that does mean that for much of the time you're paddling your canoe against the wind — hard work but it will build up your arm muscles nicely!

Small, white, fluffy clouds are blowing across the sky. The weather's fine. For now. But what about that ugly bank of gray covering the mountains beyond the end of the lake? What does that mean?

Types of cloud

1. Cirrus — wispy and high up, very widely spaced.

2. Cumulus — widely spaced and white.

3. Cumulonimbus — "anvil shape" — tall and very dark at the bottom.

4. Stratus — low, flat, and gray. They cover the whole sky.

Can you match the clouds to the following types of weather?

A. Probable drizzle.

B. Storm coming. This is a thundercloud.

C. Fine weather.

D. Fine weather, provided they stay white and widely spaced. If they are closer together and darker gray, they may bring showers.

(Answers on page 25)

A Sudden Blizzard

The weather can turn quickly in the taiga. In 1902, the Russian explorer Vladimir Arseniev was scouting along the edges of Lake Hanka in eastern Siberia with his native guide, Dersu Uzala. The weather was good but Dersu looked worried. He pointed out that the ducks and swans were flying low and quickly across the water. The two men would have to go back to their camp. "Quickly," he said. There was a bank of dark gray fog rolling toward them across the water.

Rather than heading back around the lake the way they had come, Dersu and Arseniev tried to take a shortcut through the reed beds. Soon they were stuck in a swamp. The storm hit: a snow blizzard. The temperature plummeted to well below freezing and Arseniev felt himself getting numb and then strangely sleepy in the snow flurries that lashed around him. His body had chilled and he had what is called "exposure." He would soon die unless his body warmed up. Dersu ordered him to start cutting reeds with his knife, but to leave some clumps — the corners of a square — uncut. Dersu told Arseniev to lie down. He then laid his tent canvas over the half-frozen explorer and started piling clumps of reed on top. Then he tied down the whole thing to the uncut reeds at the corners and wriggled under the canvas himself. In their makeshift shelter, the two men were able to keep out of the worst of the weather, while the clumps of reeds above them helped to keep the heat in.

Dersu and Arseniev waited out the storm for twelve hours. Most of that time Arseniev was asleep — unconscious with exposure. The time of year was early October. In the white-out of the blizzard, the two men had not realized the rest of the exploring party and their base camp were only a few hundred meters away.

But you're OK today; the weather holds all afternoon. The clouds space out and it is warm and sunny. The lake has a strange irregular shape to it, with many "fingers" that wiggle into the higher forested ground at the edges. When the snow melted in the spring, the river filled up the low-lying areas of land. The water couldn't all flow away (you'll find out why later), nor could it sink into the ground. A meter below the surface, the earth is still frozen solid with "permafrost" (like **permanent frost**).

You and Sergei, in the canoe, keep to the main lake, cutting across the mouths of the inlets where the water is often too shallow and choked with reeds to make fast progress. At one inlet, you come across an elk. It's so absorbed in feasting on waterweed that it doesn't notice you at first. Then suddenly it snorts and splashes noisily away.

ANSWERS from page 23

1. C   2. D   3. B   4. A

Remember the answers. Reading the clouds correctly may help you make the right choice later on in this trip.

The Mighty Moose
(Actually, in Siberia I'm called an elk)
The mega-herbivore of the Siberian taiga.

Favorite chomping chews: munching meadow grasses and waterweeds, stripping tree bark, and nibbling pine needles in winter.

Size: 2.1 meters tall at the shoulders.

Antlers: 2 meters across. (Only the males have antlers.) The middle bit's like a shield; the spikes are to attack other males to win a harem of females. The more spikes, the older the elk. A four-year-old with his first set of antlers may have six spikes. A fully-grown bull may have twelve. Just one problem. Living in forests, having such a huge spread on top of your head can be a little inconvenient, so after the rut (the fight for females) the antlers fall off and grow back again the next year.

Fuel requirements: Four tons of food during the winter. As it can be hard to find food under the snow, elks eat masses and masses in the summer, putting on fat that will help them last through the colder months.

A few more interesting facts:
- In winter, elks walk in their existing tracks to reduce the risk of attracting wolves.
- Elks' milk is five times richer in protein than cows' milk.
- Elks are farmed on a very small scale. The trouble is, the taiga can't support too many elks in one place because they tend to eat all the young trees and destroy the forest.

Back to your journey . . .

The long summer days mean that you can make a lot of progress while it's light, but sooner or later you'll have to set up camp. To decide where to pitch your tent, consider things like whether there is:
- Dry wood nearby for your fire
- Dry, flat ground to pitch your tent
- Fresh, clean water nearby (easy by a lake)

Luckily you soon find a suitable place. You leave Sergei to set up "house" while you gather wood and refill the water bottles. But when you come back you see it's not quite in the place you suggested. You think Sergei's made some basic mistakes. Can you spot what they are and match them up with the dangers below?

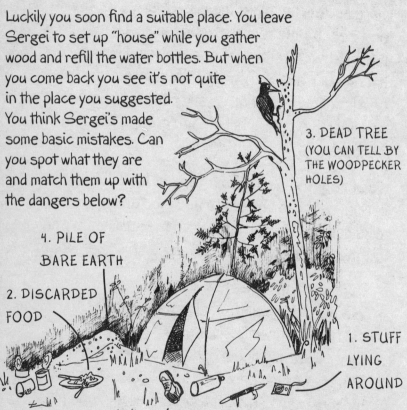

3. DEAD TREE (YOU CAN TELL BY THE WOODPECKER HOLES)

4. PILE OF BARE EARTH

2. DISCARDED FOOD

1. STUFF LYING AROUND

A. Could topple   B. Is an anthill   C. Could attract bears
D. If it snows you could lose it.

(Answers on page 31)

You decide to move your tent — and to prepare your meal
and make any waste AWAY from your campsite.
Just think of what might have
happened if you had stuck
with Sergei's plan!

Your guide does have one good idea, though.
Fishing the easy way — a night line. You leave a
fishing line with lots of baited hooks out for the
night (some
worms will do).
You might get
lucky. Get some
sleep and check
it in the morning.

Chapter 3
THE WILD RIVER

THAT NIGHT LINE is a nice idea. Unfortunately, you haven't had any luck this time, even though the bait has been nibbled off three of the hooks. Keep on trying. It's a good idea and might work some time. An easier meal might be the crayfish you see hiding under the stones in the lake shallows. They are a source of food to consider later on when your supplies are running low.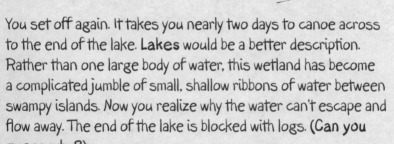

You set off again. It takes you nearly two days to canoe across to the end of the lake. **Lakes** would be a better description. Rather than one large body of water, this wetland has become a complicated jumble of small, shallow ribbons of water between swampy islands. Now you realize why the water can't escape and flow away. The end of the lake is blocked with logs. **(Can you guess why?)**

The logs stretch right across the channel, fifty meters or more. There are trunks of birch and larch trees and mud in between them, over which fresh greenery has grown up during the summer. It seems strange that all these trees have just floated here, especially as there isn't a noticeable current in the lakes. **(Got it yet?)**

Sticks and weeds float around the edges of the dam. In places, there appear to be cleared channels through the debris. **(Another clue)**.

On a bare patch of mud in a gap in the lakeside plants, there are some webbed footprints and some lumps of poop that look like they're made of wood shavings. **(Should be obvious now!)**

And now you notice the trunks of several riverside trees have been nibbled. Some have been gnawed almost right through. **(Guessed it?)**

ANSWERS to page 28

1. D   2. C   3. A   4. B

BEAVERS!

You've come to a beaver dam, a fortified lodge for a family of beavers. Five or six probably live here: an adult pair, one or two young from last year, and one or two babies from this summer. The lodge gives them shelter from the elements – even from the worst of the winter freeze, and it gives them protection from predators. No bear or wolf is going to get on that precarious pile of sticks and start digging them out or try to get in through one of the underwater entrances.

And if a predator did get in, what would it find? The largest rodent in Eurasia. The biggest recorded beavers have been one and a half meters long; that includes the flat tail that is so useful for swimming and for slapping the mud on that stick lodge.

So, why were all those trees you saw at the end of the lake nibbled? Were they all about to be felled to add to the dam? No. They're gnawed for food. The underbark of birches and willows is very nutritious — and not just for beavers. Humans can eat it too.

In fact, for surviving in the wilderness, bark is one of the most useful substances there is.

BARK!

FOOD: Fantastic flavors include birch, aspen, and willow. Best in spring when the sap is flowing. Eat the underbark raw and chew or boil it for hours. It can be roasted and ground down to make a sort of flour.

BUILDING MATERIAL: You can build a canoe with it. The classic canoes of the North-American forest Indians were made from strips of birch bark fixed and sewn over a light wooden frame. You can make baskets and boxes with smaller pieces of bark.

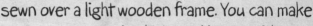

STRING: You can make lengths of string from willow bark (the inner part) by boiling it for a while with some wood ash and some of the outer bark that you scraped off to get at it. This strengthens it.

CLOTHING: You can make clothing from beaten tree bark (although this is more often done with the bark found in tropical forests than here in the taiga).

MEDICINE: And as if this wasn't enough, some tree barks when boiled with water can even be used as medicines for various ailments.

Coming across signs of
beavers was quite a
find. Beavers in Siberia
were once hunted to
the brink of extinction
for their rich, silky fur. As part
of the program to reintroduce
them, some beavers were
parachuted into remoter areas
of the taiga, in special
cages that opened when
they hit the ground.

Of course, the beaver dam
is an obstacle you have to
get the canoe past. It
means you and Sergei
taking everything out of the canoe and carrying it all in relays
around the piled-up logs to where the outflow stream starts.
Even when you get to the other side, the river is a pathetic
dribble. You end up having to drag the canoe
through the shallows for most of
the rest of the day until there's
finally enough water to
paddle in.

As you paddle on, the river becomes fast-flowing, with rocks protruding from the surface that you have to steer your way around or push away with your paddles. The front and sides of the boat are soon scraped and dented from all the collisions. Sometimes you arrive at stretches where the river barely seems to flow, and in the deep pools of cold, clear water you can see salmon darting around.

Then you round a bend and find yourself caught up in another set of rapids. The flow of the river suddenly dips down a level and you're taken with it. You need all your wits about you to keep the boat upright and you and your luggage out of the water. "Whatever happens," Sergei shouts above the roar of the river, "don't let us go side-on to the flow." He twists his hand in a gesture, which you know means the boat flipping over.

READ THE RIVER!

You have to be able to read the river. Watch the shape of the waves ahead of you. Can you guess what they mean?

1   2   3   4   5   6

WAVE SHAPE	WHAT IT MEANS AND WHAT TO DO
1. Waves in one place.	A. Whirlpool: Paddle hard and avoid if possible.
2. A V-shaped "tongue" of smooth water between rough water.	B. Rocks just underneath, go to one side.
	C. Deep water. No hazard. It's true what they say. Still waters really do run deep.
3. Choppy water (usually) behind a rounded smooth patch.	D. The main flow of the current. This is where you should run the rapid. Paddle and go straight.
4. Smooth patch, water dips down too much to see anything ahead.	E. A sudden drop in the riverbed. Often there's a "suck back." Keep straight and with the main current.
5. Still water.	
6. Like bath water going down a plughole.	F. Possible waterfall. Head to the side now and check out the river ahead.

(Answers on page 39)

If in doubt and the water looks in any way dangerous, **go to the side**. Check out the river ahead. Rapids are fun and fast but can be lethal. Realistically, an accident on a river is far more likely than the risk of animal attack on this trip. If your boat is flooded with water you could ruin all your food supplies if everything isn't well waterproofed. If your boat turns over you could lose more than your food: you could lose your life. You could hit rocks. You could drown. If you do fall out, try to end up so that your feet are facing downstream. That way you can fend off any rocks rather than hitting them head first. This is not as easy as it sounds. Capsizing in a big rapid is like being in a washing machine. After a couple of spins you have no idea which way is up or down, let alone downstream.

Remember, even if you were fine, what would happen if you lost all your gear? How would you survive?

To begin with, the rapids are sloshing slopes of water, which you scoot down with ease. At one such water chute you are concentrating so hard on keeping your canoe straight that you don't notice the shambling figure of a bear on the other side until you are nearly around the river bend. Before you can get a good look at it, the bear has ambled off into the forest.

It was probably fishing for salmon. Summer is the time of year when these fish swim from the sea up the rivers, heading for the lakes where they were born. They brave the rapids' fierce currents, even leaping up small waterfalls in their journey to their mating grounds. Male sockeye salmon, in eastern Siberia and Alaska, even change body shape.

They develop humped backs and the front of their mouths hook over so they can't even feed easily. They also turn red. All of this is to make them more attractive to the female sockeye salmon. So, the salmon reach the lakes, they mate, they spawn, then they die. All of them. It's a real food bonanza for the eagles and bears that wade in to enjoy the feast. For the adult salmon, their job is done. The thousands of eggs they have laid will soon hatch, and the young salmon will grow up and travel down to the sea. There they will live out their lives until some time in the future when they too will get the urge to return to the lake or stream of their birth and start the cycle all over again.

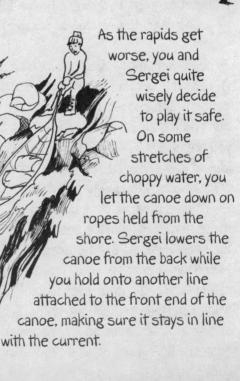

As the rapids get worse, you and Sergei quite wisely decide to play it safe. On some stretches of choppy water, you let the canoe down on ropes held from the shore. Sergei lowers the canoe from the back while you hold onto another line attached to the front end of the canoe, making sure it stays in line with the current.

Once or twice, where the river drops over a series of small waterfalls, you haul the canoe fully out, unload it, and carry everything in relays to where the water is flat again.

Eventually you reach a wide expanse of gravel and stones where another river joins from the left. Two white-tailed eagles flap into the air as you coast along the ripples where the waters meet. For the first time on the river you have a view. Dark, forested hills rise up to the north of you. Your goal, the meteorite crater, is somewhere in those hills. Getting there means setting out on foot. Here, you realize, is where you will have to leave your canoe behind.

ANSWERS to page 36

1. B   2. D   3. E   4. F   5. C   6. A

Chapter 4
THE TAIGA

YOU'VE REACHED THE fork in the river marked on the pilot's sketch map. This means it's time to abandon the canoe. You and Sergei drag it onto a bank above the river and turn it upside down so it doesn't fill up with water if it rains. You also cut some spruce branches to cover it up with. You don't want to come back in several weeks' time to find that someone's taken your only means of transportation.

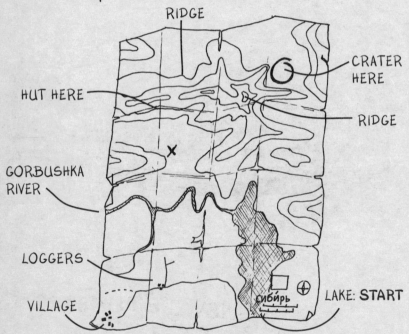

RIDGE

CRATER HERE

HUT HERE

RIDGE

GORBUSHKA RIVER

LOGGERS

VILLAGE

сибирь

LAKE: **START**

You'll be traveling on foot from now on, and you'll have to travel light. You can't possibly carry all of your stuff with you. Besides, you'll need to save some things for the journey back.

Look at the things you've taken out of your canoe. Which five should you leave here?

CANS OF FOOD

PACKAGES OF DRIED FOOD

FLARES

RIFLE AND AMMUNITION

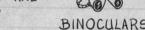

PADDLE

AXE

MED KIT

LIFE JACKET/ BUOYANCY AID

BINOCULARS

CAMP STOOLS AND TABLE

(Answers on page 43)

Your packs lightened, you and Sergei set off for the hills. At first you're weaving between the birches and willows of the riverside, but soon the conifers start. Christmas-tree-shaped larches and spruces face you on all sides. They are not so tightly packed that you can't make your way through, but they do block out a fair amount of the sunlight. As a result, the undergrowth is reduced to just clumps of mosses, lichens, and the occasional fern.

41

You have entered the taiga, a belt of mostly coniferous forest that stretches from Finland in the far northwest of Europe all the way around through northern Asia to the sea of Japan. To understand how to survive, here are some forest facts you should know.

Why are the trees Christmas-tree shaped?

So that the snow slips off easily rather than breaking the branches.

Why needles and not "normal" leaves?

Needle leaves contain little water and withstand sub-zero temperatures without freezing and becoming damaged. They also have few pores (little holes) where the tree could lose water. (In winter, it's hard for the tree to replace lost water, as everything around its roots is frozen.) Even then, some of the hardiest trees — larches — shed their needles and grow new ones in the spring.

Are all the trees evergreen? Many are, like spruces, but larches, the commonest trees in Eastern Siberia, where you find the most severe weather conditions, are deciduous. They lose their needles in winter and grow new ones in the spring.

Are all the trees coniferous?

No, but most of the most numerous and successful ones are. It just so happens that trees whose seeds are contained in cones — larches, spruces, firs, and pines — are the best-equipped to deal with this environment, because they are the right shape and have the right "leaves" to survive the harsh weather conditions.

ANSWERS from page 41

Camp stools and table — unnecessary and too bulky to carry.

Life jacket — not much point taking it, as you're not on the water any more.

Paddle — not much use without the canoe.

Binoculars — nice to take for watching the wildlife, but if you're really serious about lightening your load, leave them.

Cans of food — heavy to carry compared to dried food, but they keep better and don't need to be kept dry. Also, food in cans won't smell and attract bears. Leave it for the return journey.

How many did you get right?

0 or 1 — Useless. Work out a way to get back to the city, where you obviously belong before something awful happens to you out here in the wilderness.

2 or 3 or 4 — Mmmm, middling. You'll be rather overloaded but might make it, provided that you haven't thrown out something vital like the medical kit or the food.

All 5 — Excellent! Have you done this exploration thing before — or are you just naturally gifted at it?

And, of course, all these trees and the seeds locked up in their cones provide food for many of the herbivorous (plant-eating) animals of the taiga.

KEY

1. Chipmunks and red squirrels (actually many of the red squirrels in Siberia are black).
2. Crossbill
3. Nutcracker
4. Red-backed voles
5. Capercaillie — a turkey-sized type of grouse

Work out how each animal feeds from the tree.

A. Uses its special beak to pry open the scales of pine cones to get at the nuts inside.

B. Cracks open cones with its large beak.

C. Use their chisel-like front teeth to gnaw open cones in the trees.

D. Eats nuts on the ground but its large stomach allows it to digest young 'needles' too.

E. Nibbles open any cones that fall to the ground.

(Answers on page 50)

What about humans?
Can we eat this stuff?

Pine nuts can be eaten raw, but are better roasted. Spruce needles can be boiled up to make a sort of tea. And there's always the inner bark.

Other possibilities ...

How about **reindeer moss**, a type of lichen? It needs boiling for a long time and it isn't very nutritious. You'd need a full backpack of the stuff to give you the same food energy as a reindeer steak. But it *is* edible.

Fungi. There are lots of edible types. There are also poisonous ones. So it helps to be with someone who knows what they're looking at when it comes to eating the toadstools. Otherwise the effects could be lethal!

Fruit. Cranberries, bilberries, blackcurrants, and redcurrants can all be found in various areas of the taiga towards the end of the summer. They won't give you enough energy to survive by themselves, but they'll certainly make a tangy change to your boring trail rations.

Three days later . . .

Your rations are going down. You haven't tried the food of the forest apart from a few bilberries, which were nice but not exactly filling, and some spruce tea. This tasted not unlike pine disinfectant. You're not desperate enough to boil up tree bark or reindeer moss yet . . . and the fungi are not that appealing.

For your entire trek so far you've been following some sort of trail. When you started out at the river the path was obvious. Some of the trees had been notched with an axe. There were bare patches of ground where people had obviously walked.

Further on the signs were less obvious. Sometimes you thought you were lost but by keeping to the most logical way through the larch trees you came across signs of a trail often enough to convince yourself that this was the way you should be heading. Now, as afternoon is drawing on, the signs are there again. There are stumps of cut trees. Some show regrowth marks where they have had their bark stripped.

Then you come across a house. It's made of logs and roofed with grassy turfs. What should you do? Knock at the door? Just go in? Avoid the house and keep going?

Questions run through your mind: Who would live out here in the wilderness? Is anyone here anyway?

The cabin doesn't look in use. There are no human footprints around and the windows have been boarded up.

You decide to risk it. You push the door and go inside . . . .

Chapter 5
TRAPPERS

YOU TRY TO push open the door. It's jammed shut and needs some shoving. Inside the cabin it's dark and smells slightly moldy. There are a couple of raised platforms for beds, a log table with two chairs, and a stove made from an old oil can and some metal pipe. There are some cut logs and a bundle of dry twigs. On the table there is a box of matches with the sticks of several of them poking out, a jar containing salt, some birch bark shavings and three sticks, which someone has whittled into strange feathery shapes with a knife.

What's all the stuff here for?

"To help travelers," Sergei responds immediately. This is most likely a trappers' hut. The hut's owner is probably away hunting. He's left his hut how he would like to find one if he were lost and cold in the wilderness. That's the tradition around here.

Travelers' Etiquette

1. Why are the matches sticking out of the box?

A. To keep them dry.

B. So that someone with fingers numb from cold can strike them.

C. So that they are harder to lose.

2. What are the feather sticks for?

A. To help light fires.

B. They are ornaments.

C. They are charms to ward off evil spirits.

3. The birch shavings, the twigs, and the cut logs are all for lighting fires. Which order would you set light to them?

A. Light the bark shavings (tinder) to light the twigs (kindling) to light the logs (fuel).

B. Light the twigs (kindling) to light the bark shavings (tinder) to light the logs (fuel).

C. Light the logs (fuel) to light the bark shavings (tinder) to light the twigs (kindling).

4. Should you feel free to use all this stuff?

A. No. It's someone else's property. You should leave it alone and leave the hut as you found it.

B. Yes. Feel free to use what you want.

C. Yes, but replace what you use. Leave the hut as you found it.

(Answers on page 53)

Soft Gold

Hunting animals for their fur was what the exploration of Siberia was all about. "Soft Gold," they called it. The forests were vast and, with the winters being so cold, many of the animals that lived there had silky coats. Years ago (and in some parts of the world even today), many people though these furs would look — and feel — good as coats or hats. In big cities like London and Paris, wearing a dead animal on your head or a "stole" wrapped around your neck (for ladies) was the height of fashion. One animal in particular was prized: the sable. A member of the weasel family, not unlike a small, dark pine marten, sables had the silkiest furs, especially in winter when they were super soft and fleecy. The trouble was getting the furs undamaged. A gun shot could ruin a fur worth as much as the number of bars of silver it could be filled with. To solve the problem, the Russian colonists got the local people, the Tungus and Samoyeds, the Yakuts and Kamchadels, to do the dirty work. (They also forced the native people to pay a tax, called Yasak, to the Russian authorities to live in the forests where they had lived for generations.)

They had the skill to shoot an arrow or a rifle bullet through the sable's nose or eye, avoiding damaging the precious fur. Sometimes the hunters made traps: they used a hole in a tree, which the inquisitive sable would then poke its head into, only to get a heavy weight come crashing down on it when it pushed a hidden trip wire. With all this hunting, sables soon became virtually extinct in many areas, and the hunters switched their attention to other furry animals. Squirrels, foxes, beavers — every pelt brought in good money. As the animals ran out, the hunters moved ever eastward in search of new hunting grounds. It was these hunters and trappers, not explorers on expeditions, who first explored the vast empty taiga.

ANSWERS to page 44

1. C   2. A   3. B   4. E   5. D

After one night's stay at the trappers' hut, you and Sergei set off again. You make sure to leave the cabin just as you found it — and just as you hope to find it again on your journey back.

The land is starting to rise now as the trail takes you into the hills. The trees are not as tall and are more spaced out. There are patches over open ground with clumps of mosses, bilberry bushes, and dwarf "stone" pine trees. The air definitely has a cold nip to it, though whether this is because of your height above the river valley or a change in the weather, you don't know. Sergei thinks there's a snowstorm coming. Look at the clouds. What do you think?

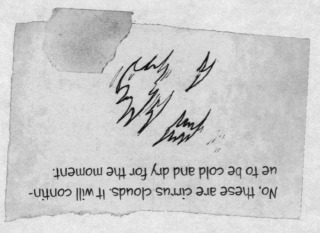

No, these are cirrus clouds. It will continue to be cold and dry for the moment.

Sergei is wrong this time, but he could have been right— in this climate the weather can change unpredictably. Snow on the ground would mean you losing your trail into the hills. For the animals, it could lose them the chance of finding food. In a couple more months, the days will be getting shorter and the temperatures lower.

What will these different animals do when winter comes?

1. Redwing

2. Sable

3. Brown bear

4. Siberian jay

5. Elk

6. Wolverine

A. Semi-hibernate. Finds itself a cozy cave, blocks up most of the entrance with sticks, and leaves and sleeps its way through the worst of the cold weather.

B. Migrates to England and western Europe, where the winters are milder.

C. Lives on a store of nuts that it has previously hidden under the bark of trees.

D. Plunges under the snow to hunt voles and lemmings out of their burrows, as it's unable to snack on the cranberries that normally form part of its diet.

E. Changes diet and starts nibbling at tree bark and pine needles.

F. Hunts down half-starved, weakened animals.

(Answers on page 54)

And the small animals? The wood lemmings and voles? They cope as well as they can under the snow, nibbling grass roots and any old seeds they can find until the spring thaw comes. And if you think it's safe under the snow, think again. These small animals have the supersonic hearing of the great gray owl to contend with: it can hear the slightest movement as much as a meter under the snow. What's more, the owl's softened feathers muffle the sound of its wing beats as it hovers in the air, so there is no warning for these poor little mites. The owl will home in on its target and plunge into the snow. These are effective tactics, yes, but not enough to wipe out the lemming population completely. Once the winter's gone they'll be back, breeding fast. Lemmings are responsible for a regular yearly population explosion — and a time of plenty for all the owls and other predators that feed on them.

ANSWERS to page 48

1. B   2. A   3. A   4. C

This is how the lemming population explosion works. A pair of wood lemmings survive the winter.... They breed.... Twenty days later up to twelve babies are born.... These grow up and are ready to breed in only nineteen days!

So if each of the twelve lemmings finds a mate and has twelve kids, work it out....
12 x 12 = 144 babies in as little as twenty more days.
In 39 days the original pair of lemmings could have 144 grandchildren.

What's more, the original pair may have had another litter of twelve young in the meantime. In fact, they'll probably produce three litters in the summer season, and some of these children might also have children in that time. Pretty soon the whole forest floor could be alive with lemming children, grandchildren and great grandchildren, all swarming around nibbling at pine cones ... if it wasn't for...

ANSWERS from page 52
1. B 2. D 3. A 4. C (nutcrackers do this too)
5. E 6. F

Predators!

The sables, weasels, and owls can have a field day — the lemmings providing the food for them to raise their own young. But, and this is the important thing, the predators never get all the lemmings. There are always enough to survive the winter and start the cycle again.

Remember, predators in the taiga come in different sizes. There are plenty that are big enough to take you on! Unlike the lemmings who breed themselves out of danger (by being so numerous that they can never all be caught), there's only one of you. That is something to think about when you make camp and you hear the wolves howling tonight. Find out more about them in the next chapter. . . .

Chapter 6
PREDATORS OF THE TAIGA

WOLVES! YOU CAN hear two packs howling in the cold night air. One group (the louder one) is ahead of you. Their yips and yowls are being answered by

other wolves back in the direction you've come from. It's hard to tell how far away either pack is. Wolf calls travel for miles. Just for your own peace of mind, you and Sergei bank up the fire so that it's really blazing before you turn in for the night.

The thought of wolves makes you shudder. You've heard all the stories — "Little Red Riding Hood," "The Three Little Pigs," "Werewolves." Everyone knows wolves are vicious killers.
But are they?

Maybe wolves have just gotten a bad rep!

The Wolf: a misunderstood carnivore

Here are a few facts you might already know ...

- Wolves are the top predators of the taiga.
- They like eating reindeer and elk but will go for anything else if it's an easy meal — rabbits, birds, farm animals like sheep.
- Wolves hunt in packs. In an area where there is lots of large prey, like elks, a wolf pack may number fifty or more animals, but most packs are much smaller.

- The pack is lead by an "alpha male." He is top dog. All the other wolves are submissive (look up) to him.
- Wolves scent-mark their trails using poop and pee. Only the boss males cock their leg up to pee a scent mark!
- Wolves have a strong sense of smell. Their sight is also good, although at long distances they can only detect movement. Wolves do not see in color.

- Wolves howl to bring their pack together and to declare to any other packs nearby that this is their territory — "Keep away!"
- Every wolf knows his or her place in the pack. They have different ways of expressing this in their body language. (You will probably have seen dogs do the same thing — remember, all dogs are descended from wolves.)

HEAD DOWN.
HARD STARE.
TEETH SHOWING.
GROWL.
"I'M THE BOSS.
GOT IT?"

TAIL BETWEEN LEGS.
"YOU REALLY ARE THE BOSS
AND I'M SUCH A FOOL. I GROVEL
TO YOU, O, MASTER."

ROLLING ON BACK,
LEGS IN AIR. THROAT
SHOWING.
"I TRUST YOU SO
MUCH YOU COULD
BITE MY THROAT
OUT IF YOU
REALLY WANTED.
I JUST WANT TO BE
APPRECIATED."

Here are a few more facts you should know.

- To keep a pack supplied with food, wolves need a huge territory to roam in: hundreds of square kilometers. So, packs of wolves are spread out very far apart in the taiga.

- Wolves actually rarely go for farm animals if there are good numbers of elk and deer in the area ... but be realistic: who's going to pass up an easy meal of a slow-moving sheep if there happens to be one in your hunting range?

- Thousands of wolves are killed each year by people.

- Wolves only rarely attack humans. They've been hunted for so long that they know to keep out of their way.

- Wolves keep down the numbers of elks and large deer – like wapiti. In the USA, wolves have been reintroduced into some areas to control deer, which have become a nuisance, stripping all the young trees and destroying the forest (as well as peoples' gardens!).

Wolves are big, fierce predators. The trouble is that so much fear has grown up around them that they've been wiped out in most of the areas they naturally lived in, like western Europe and much of the USA. Now they are nearly all found in the most remote wilderness areas. Wolves aren't bad. They are just misunderstood.

Wolves aren't the only predators in the forest. Here's a short quiz to test you on what you know about some of the others. A few of the answers are mentioned in the previous chapter. Some are common sense.

Predators in the taiga: TRUE or FALSE?

1. The brown bear is the biggest carnivore in the taiga.
2. Sables hunt in packs.
3. Wolves were nearly driven to extinction by hunters after their silky fur coats.
4. Wolves doze through much of the winter.
5. In North America, brown bears are called grizzly bears.

6. Lynxes are quick to give up the chase when hunting arctic hares, as the hares are too small to be worth the effort.
7. Wolverines' big feet stop them sinking into soft snow, which gives them more of a chance of catching deer in winter.
8. Wolverines have been known to take on reindeer when they are really hungry.

(Answers on page 63)

Wolves, bears, wolverines, even tigers! Is the taiga swarming with carnivores?

NO. The fact is that unlike a tropical rainforest, there is little food further down the food chain that is available to these animals. Not many animals eat spruce, larch, or pine needles, and large herbivores, like elk and reindeer, that forage for lichen and tree bark have to roam large distances just to get enough to keep themselves going. And this is especially true in winter, when plant food is very scarce. The carnivores that eat the herbivores are very spread out.

Each wolf pack needs hundreds of square kilometers in which to find enough food. Wolverines are constantly wandering in search of an easy meal, which is very hard to find. Other carnivores, like bears, foxes, and sables, have to supplement their diet with nuts and berries. So, because these carnivores have to scavenge for food over such a large area, your chances of seeing a wolf, lynx, or wolverine are very slim indeed. (You should count yourself very lucky if you do spot one!) But if you do happen to have a close encounter, this is what you should do. . . .

WOLVERINES would most likely keep well away from you, but if you found one in winter with a reindeer or some other carcass, don't mess with it.

WOLVES are most dangerous if you're injured and alone. You could drive wolves off by shouting, or with fire or a warning shot from your gun. Wolves can't climb trees. But can you?

BEARS – meeting one of these fellows is a far more likely proposition, especially if you're stupid enough to leave food around your camp – the bear will have come to eat that, not you. Your best bet, if you see it before it sees you, is to keep out the way, especially if it's a mother with cubs. You could try to drive it off with a warning shot or by shouting, but never get within reach of a swipe from those huge claws.

Back off, and when you are far enough away, run as fast as you can, zigzagging if possible.

- Don't try to play dead. It won't work.
- A bear's most sensitive part is the end of its nose. You could hit it there, but are you really stupid enough to try getting that close?
- Make a noise while you are walking on a trail. Some people wear special bear bells. That way the bear hears you coming and moves out the way.

1. T. A really big bear can weigh 750 Kg, as much as ten men.
2. F. Wolves do.
3. F. Sables were.
4. F. That's bears.
5. T.

SABLE

6. T. A lynx would put more effort into hunting a deer which gives far more meat. Incidentally, lynxes aren't the only big cats in the taiga. In the far east of Siberia there are several hundred tigers left. Siberian tigers are the biggest type of tiger. They are seriously endangered by hunting and forest destruction.
7. T. Wolverines usually eat carrion (dead animals), but in winter they have been known to make a quick dash and catch reindeer.
8. T. The other name for this animal is a glutton, which means someone who eats a lot.

Your trek through the taiga with Sergei continues...

Three days from the hunters' cabin, you know you must be getting closer to the meteorite crater. But there is no sign of it yet: there is no change in the vegetation—where the trees grew back after the impact; there is no sign of the magnetic anomalies that the pilot who found the crash site reported; and your compass works fine.

In this thick forest, for all you know, you could have passed your destination without realizing. Where is that Uncle Vlad whom Sergei promised you would find? It's cold, you are tired, and the trail is getting hard to follow again. What's more, the Cumulus clouds are building up ahead of you, and you know what that means....

Storm coming!

You can feel the wind gusting through the larches. The treetops are swaying and occasionally loose branches thud to the floor. Then the snow starts, a few flurries at first, then a swirling mass of white. You need to find shelter. Now! Sergei's your guide. He should know what to do, you grumble as you trudge along. You turn to tell him what you think, but he's not there...

A sickening thought hits the pit of your stomach.

YOU ARE ALONE!

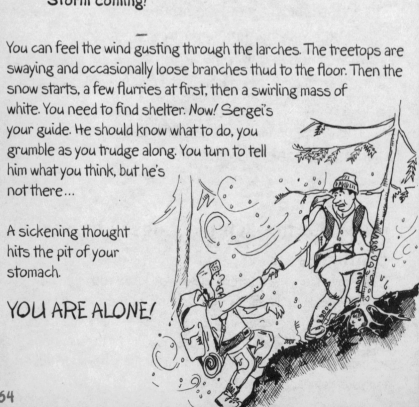

Chapter 7
THE TUNGOYEDS

THE TEMPERATURE HAS now dropped below freezing. It's snowing; you are alone in the forest with the wolves and the bears, not with your guide. He's lost out there. Somewhere. To make things worse: he has the gun; he has the tent. You shout but get no response. This is a survival situation. You must decide what to do. *Now!* Before you get too cold.

ALONE: Quick Quiz

1. What is your first need?
A. Food
B. Fire
C. Shelter
D. Water

2. What could you use to keep the snow off?
A. Spruce branches
B. Piled-up snow
C. Tree trunks

3. What is your second need?
A. Food
B. Fire
C. Shelter
D. Water

4. Should you try and find Sergei first before you do anything else?
A. Yes. You stand a better chance together.
B. No. You could get more lost.

(Answers on page 66)

1. C.
2. A (not enough snow for a snow cave – yet!).
3. B (You must keep warm).
4. B.

Here's how you can improvise a quick shelter using your hatchet and a nearby spruce tree.

- Cut down a fairly narrow tree at about head height.
- Cut away the branches underneath.
- Lay these on the ground to make an insulating floor.
- Crawl inside.

Once you're under cover, you can chip away some wood for your fire. In this cold, lighting a fire may be difficult. So prepare the tinder, kindling, and fuel carefully before you start.

If you have the time and energy to make it, a screen made out of more branches like this will reflect some of the fire's heat back to you.

You huddle into your shelter and warm yourself as best you can. In the whiteout you are suddenly aware of dim shapes looming out of the falling snow. Wolf-sized shapes.

You hear a sound, like tin cans rattling together. These wolves have antlers. . . .

REINDEER!

And they obviously belong to someone. Many are wearing collars — the rattling was the tinkling of the homemade bells tied around their necks.

A smaller animal appears through the falling snow — a dog. It stops and starts barking and growling. This is your most dangerous animal encounter yet. You could easily get bitten. You back off, pressing yourself further into your tree shelter. You hope the dog's owner turns up soon.

You hear a whistle and the dog turns away. There are two people in front of you. One is Sergei — looking very relieved. The other is a Mongolian-looking man with a huge coat and a fur hat with earflaps pulled tight around his face.

"This is Uncle Vladimir." Sergei introduces you. "He's from the Tungoyed tribe. The rest of his brigade [the name of the group] are nearby and can help us."

Siberia. It's not the first place that comes to mind when you think of tribes. You're more likely to think of the Amazon rainforest. Nonetheless, there are still tribal people — like the Tungus and the Yakuts — living in small groups in the vast areas of the taiga and the barren tundra to the north. Many live and work in towns and villages, but a few still live by hunting, trapping, and herding reindeer.

THESE ARE THE SORTS OF CLOTHES A SIBERIAN FOREST TRIBESMAN WOULD TRADITIONALLY WEAR.

If you think a North-American Indian might look pretty similar, there are a couple of reasons for this:

1. Across the Pacific Ocean in Canada and Alaska there are forests which are very much like those of the Siberian taiga. Tribes there live in the same conditions and use similar clothing and tools.

2. American Indians are related to the original Siberians. Ten thousand years ago, during the last ice age, sea levels were lower and Alaska was joined on to Siberia where the Bering Strait is today. The first people to arrive on the American continent were the Siberians, who crossed the icy waste of the Bering "land bridge," then spread out south to populate the new land they had found.

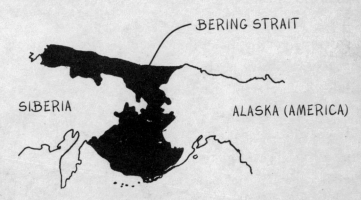

BERING STRAIT

SIBERIA

ALASKA (AMERICA)

What do tribal Siberians look like today? It depends what they're wearing, of course!!! Jackets, T-shirts, jeans — anything. However, in the cold sub-arctic winter, there is still nothing better than reindeer fur, and many still wear that. (By the way, the fur is worn on the inside to trap a layer of insulating air.)

The shaman and their drums

Religious life for the Siberian tribes revolves around the witch doctor or shaman. Shaman were usually, but not always, men. In some areas the shaman were transvestites; they wore the clothes and took on the habits of the opposite sex. These "soft men" were said to have special "spirit" helpers or supernatural "husbands." Every shaman used a round ritual drum to enter a deep trance where he could communicate with "the ancestors" and ask for advice or help to heal a sick person. In the Tungus tribe the drum's rim was cut from a living larch tree to keep it bound up with the life of the forest. Sometimes the drum had a carving of the shaman's spirit helper on one of the crosspieces. Supernatural fantasy maybe, but maybe not. Lots of people in towns and villages all over Siberia still go to visit a shaman, not a doctor, when they are ill.

Uncle Vlad's settlement is only a short walk through the trees. There are three large tents that look like Indian tepees. You are bundled into the nearest one, cozily warm from the heat of a wood-burning stove in its center. You are given a bowl full of meaty soup, and the warmth, combined with your exhaustion, sends you to sleep within minutes.

Morning . . .

Everyone around you is in a flurry of activity. Tepees are being pulled down and the skin coverings rolled up. Cooking pots, bedding, even babies (wrapped up against the cold), are being strapped onto reindeer, ready to set off. Vlad says the brigade is striking camp and heading off to find better pasture for the reindeer. The three families with their hundred or so reindeer have to move on every few weeks. That way the lichen the reindeer live on doesn't get totally grazed away, and there will still be enough to grow back for next year when the brigade may return.

Vlad explains that some years ago the government made the herders keep all their reindeer in one place. The results were disastrous for the reindeer, which ran out of food ... but not so disastrous for all the local wolves.

The brigade is virtually self-sufficient. Nearly everything the families need comes from either the reindeer or the forest.

Reindeer provide meat and milk (the milk is fifteen times fattier than cows milk). Their hides are used to make clothes, shoes, and tents. Their sinews are useful for making tough threads to bind or sew things together.

Other food comes from the forest: fish can be caught in the lakes, and there is usually fruit — like bilberries — to be picked. Once in a while a government helicopter brings in essential medicines and takes the older children to or from boarding school in the city. But for most of the time, the Tungoyeds are here alone. They can go for months on end without meeting other people.

Uncle Vlad says he would be happy to guide you and Sergei to the crater, but there's really no need: it is less than a day's walk away and he can show you a trail that will take you all the way. He'll be taking the brigade in another direction, to where the grazing is better.

Mammoths

Before you set off, Vlad shows you something he found recently. It's a mammoth tusk. And it doesn't look old.

But mammoths are extinct right? They died out around the end of the last ice age, ten thousand years ago. So where is this tusk from...?

Well, there are rumors that they are still alive and well, surviving in the Siberian forests. There is tons of room and virtually no people, so they might have gone unnoticed. But how likely is that? Mammoths are pretty big after all.

But if it isn't a new tusk, why is it so well-preserved? The reason is it's been deep-frozen. A meter or two under the ground there is permafrost. If a mammoth died thousands of years ago and sank into a swamp that then froze hard, pieces or sometimes all of the mammoth would have been prevented from rotting.

This is what must have happened to thousands of mammoths because many tusks have been found in excellent condition. In fact, at one point, so many tusks were discovered there was a flourishing ivory business that, like the sable fur hunting, made some Siberians very rich. But it wasn't just tusks that were found: whole, deep-frozen mammoths have been discovered, still with their hair on. Some were partly eaten away by wolves; here was meat that was perhaps twenty thousand years past its sell-by date.

More recently, scientists have been looking at ways to extract DNA from mammoth remains. Though the technology isn't advanced enough at present, it may be possible one day to re-create a living, breathing mammoth!

Back on the trail ...

Uncle Vlad's "less than a day's walk" is a real killer, you discover. It's all up and down and hard on your knees and leg muscles. The forest is thick, dark, and dreary, and the trail blocked by frequent tree falls. Everything is still and quiet. Not even the wildlife seems to like this part of the forest — apart from the midges and mosquitoes. They are truly horrendous here. Whenever you stop, your faces and hands soon become covered with biting flies. The only way to avoid them is to carry on without having any rests.

Eventually your path starts to rise again and the trees begin to thin out. Just when you are feeling more miserable and done-in by the day you make it to the top of a barren ridge. And this is the view you see....

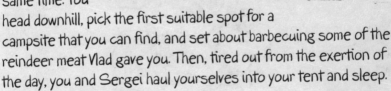

The bowl is filled with larch trees that all look about the same height. They must have grown at the same time. You head downhill, pick the first suitable spot for a campsite that you can find, and set about barbecuing some of the reindeer meat Vlad gave you. Then, tired out from the exertion of the day, you and Sergei haul yourselves into your tent and sleep.

You feel a vague sense of unease that you have forgotten to do something important, but you put it out of your mind as sleep takes hold of you.

What did you forget to do?

Chapter 8
METEORITE CRATER

SNUFFLING, HEAVY BREATHING, right next to your face. Not Sergei. He is still asleep in the tent next to you. The noise is from outside. And it's close. The meat! You left the reindeer meat over the fire and your gun is propped up on a tree stump nearby.

More snuffling and snorting. **THERE'S A BEAR OUT THERE!**
This is a plan view of your camp.

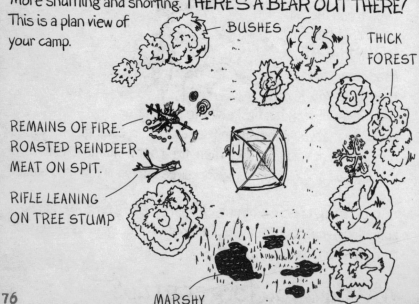

BUSHES

THICK FOREST

REMAINS OF FIRE.
ROASTED REINDEER
MEAT ON SPIT.

RIFLE LEANING
ON TREE STUMP

MARSHY

WHAT DO YOU DO NEXT?

Start with 100 Life points. You need a coin for this: some answers will be decided by throwing the coin. Each answer may lose you points. If you drop below zero, you've had it and the bear's got you. There are NO completely right answers, but some are better than others.

QUESTION 1
You weigh your options. What are they?
A. Stay perfectly still. **GO TO QUESTION 2**
B. Shoot the bear. **GO TO QUESTION 3**
C. Fire a warning shot at the bear. **GO TO QUESTION 3**
D. Carefully unzip your tent, then leg it. **GO TO QUESTION 3**
E. Use your penknife to cut your way out the back of the tent. **GO TO QUESTION 4**

QUESTION 2
At least you didn't go toward the bear. No points lost yet. But have you noticed you've still got food out in the porch of your tent? Do you want to reconsider what to do?

A. Use your penknife to cut your way out of the back of the tent. **GO TO QUESTION 4**

B. Continue staying perfectly still and do absolutely nothing. **GO TO QUESTION 5**

QUESTION 3

You are now outside the tent. There is a large brown bear snuffling through the remains of last night's meal. He has noticed you. **(-30 points).**

What do you want to do now?

A. Run away. **GO TO QUESTION 7**
B. Run toward the bear shouting. **GO TO QUESTION 9**
C. Try to grab the gun. **GO TO QUESTION 10**
D. Back away quietly, trying to show as little fear as possible. **GO TO QUESTION 8**

QUESTION 4

You're outside the tent. You can't see the bear but you can hear the snuffling breathing coming toward you. **(-20 points).**

What now?

A. Run away. **GO TO QUESTION 7**
B. Stay still. **GO TO QUESTION 6**
C. Back away quietly. **GO TO QUESTION 8**

QUESTION 5

You stay still for what seems an age. The scuffling noises move toward you. The bear is investigating the porch of the tent. Its nose is stuck under the fly sheet and there is just the thin cloth of the inner tent separating you from it. **(-50 points).**

A. Stay still. **GO TO QUESTION 6**

B. Use your penknife to cut your way out of the back of the tent. **GO TO QUESTION 7**

QUESTION 6

Throw a coin.

HEADS: the bear ignores you and moves off. You survived.

TAILS: The bear smelled you or heard your breathing. Your only option is escape. (If you are still in the tent, you will have to cut the tent fabric and wriggle out). **GO TO QUESTION 4**

QUESTION 7

The bear is bounding after you. **(-40 points).**

Will you survive? **GO TO QUESTION 8**

QUESTION 8

Throw a coin.

HEADS: the bear ignores you and you get away.

TAILS: the bear notices you and is coming your way (**-30 points**). Your options:

A. Run away. **GO TO QUESTION 7**

B. Run towards the bear shouting. **GO TO QUESTION 9**

C. Carry on backing off. **GO TO QUESTION 8 (again)**

D. Play dead. **GO TO QUESTION 10**

QUESTION 9

This is stupid enough to work. Maybe. Throw a coin.

HEADS: You chased it off.

TAILS. (-50 points). If you are still alive. **GO TO QUESTION 8**

QUESTION 10

Stupid, as it's already seen you (and knows what you're up to). **(-80 points)**.

Did you survive? Let's hope so. The fact is that many potentially dangerous situations in the wilderness can be avoided with just a little forethought and preparation — like hiding fresh meat away from your camp when there are large carnivores around.

Bears aren't man-eaters. It's just that they'll feed on any easy meal: roots, fruit, insect grubs, wild honey, or even an elk if they can get close enough without being noticed. Most of the real dangers in the taiga are far less obvious than animal attack. You're probably in more danger from the risk of exposure to the cold, or from injuries like a broken leg. Remember, if you get sick in the wilderness, there is no medical help available.

THE BEAR . . . takes the scraps of meat and, after trashing your camp in search of any other tasty morsels, ambles off. When you judge that the coast is clear, you and Sergei return, gather up your stuff and continue down into the crater.

The trees here are virtually all narrow-trunked larches. They probably started growing shortly after the original tree cover was blown flat in the meteorite explosion. That was nearly a hundred years ago. The fact that the trees are so thin shows how slowly things grow in this cold northern forest. The larches block out much of the light reaching the forest floor and this is bare apart from a thin fuzz of mosses and lichens.

As you shuffle through the lichen at the bottom of the crater, your foot kicks a piece of strange black object about the size of your fist. You pick it up. It's remarkably heavy, more like a piece of metal than a rock.

When you rub away the dirt covering it, you can see it's slightly shiny and has rippled markings, almost like fingerprints pressed into clay. What's more, it attracts the needle of your compass. This "rock" must be part of the meteorite that blew out the crater.

Here's why:
— Many meteorites contain iron and nickel — metals that are heavy and attracted to magnets (like your compass needle).
— Many meteorites are shiny where the bare metal is showing or where they have melted upon entering Earth's atmosphere.
— Fingerprint patterns, called "regmaglypts," are found on some, but not all, meteorites.

So, you've made it. Your theory about there being a meteorite impact crater in the middle of the Siberian wilderness was right.

And you have evidence too. That lump of heavy black rock should help convince people of your discovery when you get back. You'll be a scientific superstar! You'll be asked to give lectures at the most important universities.

You'll almost certainly be on the TV and radio news, and in the newspapers. "How did you do it?" they'll ask. "How did you deal with the bears and the wolves?" "Weren't you ever tempted to give up and come back home?" "Who helped you? Is it true that Sergei and Uncle Vladimir will be setting up their own tour agency to guide adventurers to the heart of the taiga? And how do I sign up for one of their trips?"

JOURNEY HOME

Fame and fortune await you when you get home. But that's still a long way off. You still have to get back. Can you remember the way you came?

Look at the map opposite and list, in order, the nine hexagons that made up your route.

(Answers are on page 87)

Here are some hints.

You and Sergei traveled by logging truck to the lake. You canoed to the end, where there was a beaver dam. You rode the rapids down the river until you came to an open area where another river joined. Then you struck out on foot, first on a trail, which led to a hunters' cabin, then across the taiga, where you could hear wolves howling at night. After Uncle Vlad rescued you and took you to his brigade's encampment, it was a short trek through the hills to the crater.

It's time to head home until the next adventure. You've proved yourself to be a skilled explorer of the northern wilderness, but why stop there? What new challenges await you? Try a new adventure: *In the Jungle, Under the Sea, On Safari, On the South Sea Islands, In the Himalayas, In the Desert,* and *At the North Pole.*

EXPLORERS WANTED!

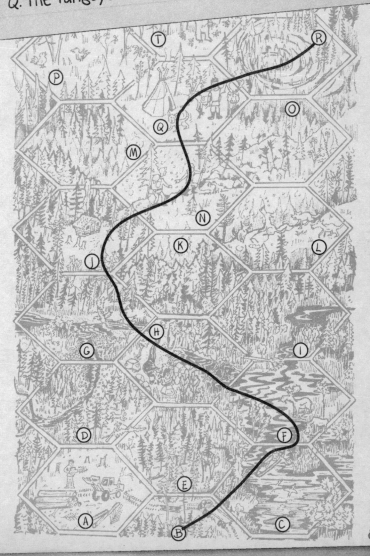

ANSWERS to page 83

B. Loggers truck   C. & F. Lake   H. & G. River

J. Hunters' cabin   N. Across the taiga

Q. The Tungoyeds camp   R. The meteorite crater

Your mission...

should you choose to accept it,
is to lead an expedition through the Amazon
in search of a "lost city."

Are you ready for the challenge?

Explorers Wanted to:

- Endure sweltering heat
- Battle ravenous ants
- Meet Indian tribes
- Handle poisonous snakes
- Brave jungle diseases

Includes the author's own expedition notes and sketches!

EXPLORERS
WANTED!

IN THE JUNGLE

Simon Chapman

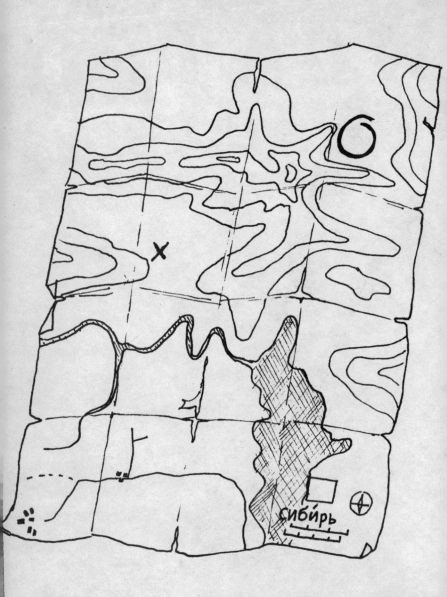

СИБИРЬ

SO ... YOU WANT TO BE A JUNGLE EXPLORER?

You want to wander in the deepest, darkest jungles
in the heart of the Amazon rainforest where
NO ONE has ever gone before?

You want to find ...

Lost Cities ... Tribes ... ?

Weird and wonderful creatures ... ?

If the answer to any of these questions is **YES**,
then this is the book for you. Read on....

THIS BOOK GIVES you the lowdown on life in the Amazon rainforest and essential tips for your expedition, like how to get there, what to take, and **what to expect.** There are also some pretty scary true-life stories of people who have tried to explore it before ... so read on!

YOUR MISSION

... SHOULD YOU CHOOSE TO ACCEPT IT, IS TO MOUNT AN EXPEDITION THROUGH THE RAINFOREST IN SEARCH OF THE RUINS OF A LOST CITY, WHICH IS SAID TO LIE IN THE MOUNTAINOUS HEADWATERS OF THE RIO VENOMOSO, THE "POISONOUS RIVER." THE NAMWEYOS TRIBE OF INDIANS WHO LIVE IN THE REGION HAVE LONG TOLD STORIES OF STONE BUILDINGS DEEP IN THE JUNGLE. THEY CALL THE RUINS "RUCU-RUMIMARCA," WHICH MEANS "OLD CITY OF STONE" IN THE ANCIENT LANGUAGE OF THE QUECHUA PEOPLE OF THE HIGHLANDS. THE NAMWEYOS SAY THE SPIRITS OF THE DEAD HAUNT THE RUINS. CHEWED BONES HAVE BEEN FOUND AMONG THE OVERGROWN STONEWORK, AND A LOW-PITCHED GROWLING HAS OFTEN BEEN HEARD THERE AT NIGHT. BECAUSE OF THIS, THE INDIANS WILL NOT GO NEAR THE PLACE.

IS RUCU-RUMIMARCA ALL
THAT REMAINS OF SOME
LONG-LOST CIVILIZATION?

ARE THERE ARCHAEOLOGICAL
TREASURES TO BE FOUND?

MAYBE THERE'S GOLD!

IT'S UP TO YOU
TO FIND OUT.

YOU WILL HAVE TO JOURNEY THROUGH UNEXPLORED
RAINFOREST TO GET THERE — BY RIVER AND THEN
ON FOOT OVERLAND — CLIMBING UP INTO THE
MISTY RIDGES WHERE THE CITY IS SAID TO BE
LOCATED. THERE YOU WILL HAVE TO MAKE CONTACT
WITH THE SECRETIVE NAMWEYOS, WHOSE HELP YOU
WILL NEED IF YOU ARE TO DISCOVER THE
MYSTERIOUS CITY OF STONE.

Time to set the scene...

Let's find out some vital facts about the rainforest before the mission gets underway.

The Amazon rainforest is HUGE. In fact, it's an area of trees, swamps, and rivers the size of Europe. If it's hard to imagine how really vast that is, picture your neighborhood covered in trees, then your town, city, or county. THEN imagine that all the way to the farthest place you've been to in a car is forest and rivers, and hardly any roads. Well, that would still only be a tiny part of how big the Amazon is. It is just awesome!

PLANET EARTH

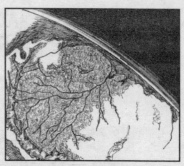

SOUTH AMERICA:
THE AMAZON BASIN

The Amazon rainforest in South America is not the only place where rainforests grow. Here are some other places around the world where tropical jungles can be found.

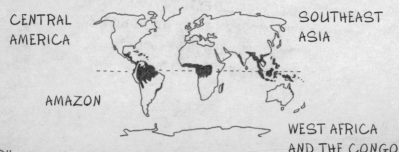

CENTRAL
AMERICA

SOUTHEAST
ASIA

AMAZON

WEST AFRICA
AND THE CONGO

Zooming in on the Amazon . . .

The Amazon is like a maze of rivers, snaking across the land in sweeping, wide twists. From the air, the rainforest looks like broccoli!

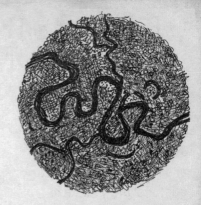

THE AMAZON RIVER

ZOOMING IN STILL CLOSER . . .

to one muddy river bend on a minor tributary, deep in the jungle . . .

But what's it like under the cover of the trees?

Everywhere you look, there are leaves and tree trunks. Most of the trunks are thin and tall. Their tops branch out far above your head. This is called the canopy. The leaves here block out most of the sunlight, so everything appears quite dim. Your camera won't work without a flash and direct sunshine only lights up a few small patches.

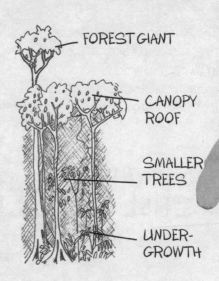

FOREST GIANT

CANOPY ROOF

SMALLER TREES

UNDER-GROWTH

The ground is covered with undergrowth — small bushes, ferns, and palm trees. Although this is thick in places, it is usually possible to push through without too much difficulty. There are also long, twisted, leafy vines that dangle from some of the trees and snake out along the ground.

Occasionally, you come across a tree trunk that is truly enormous; it's propped up from falling over by buttress roots that trail off in all directions.

BUTTRESS ROOTS

Underneath the canopy, the air is hot and humid. It's not steamy exactly, but feels sticky. You begin to feel very sweaty and damp. Everything smells moldy (and so will you if you stay long enough). Fungus sticks out from dead branches and the tree trunks are blotchy with lichen. Many of the leaves even look moldy and nibbled at, perhaps by caterpillars or maybe by leaf-cutter ants. These ants are probably the first sign of animal life that you notice. They march in long lines across the forest floor, each carrying a piece of leaf, like a tiny green sail, to their nest. Here the ants feed the leaf pieces to a fungus which they eat. There are many other insects around — like blue morpho butterflies the size of your hand. Their wings reflect light when the sun hits them, but when they are closed the back of the wings are camouflaged to look like dead leaves. You'll also be tracked down by mosquitoes that will home in on the carbon dioxide in your breath. They hover around your face and arms, attacking whenever you stand still — sinking their mouth spikes through your shirt and sucking your blood! Unless you are wearing repellent, you will soon have itchy red bumps wherever they've managed to get through — NASTY!

Control	Setting	Level
SOUND FX	insects, birds	▭——— MAX
BRIGHTNESS	dim, shady	▭— MAX
SMELLINESS	rotten, moldy	▭————— MAX
COLOR	green, some brown	▭———— MAX

Apart from insects, you probably won't see much wildlife at first, but it'll be there, hiding out of sight in the canopy above your head, or maybe in the undergrowth just in front of you.

Suddenly, there is a rustle of leaves ahead of you...

You push forward, past a tree trunk with lots of thorny roots...

You try to keep as quiet as possible and listen out for more movement...

Anything could be behind that next tree...

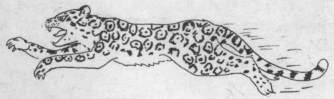

A jaguar...

Kills by biting through the skull.

A giant anaconda . . .

Smothers its prey.

A vampire bat . . .

A real problem when you are asleep. It shaves off a slice of skin from your thumb or big toe and sucks on your blood. You don't feel a thing as vampire bats have anaesthetic spit!

SO . . . you creep forward through the undergrowth, past some overhanging leaves . . .

WHAT DO YOU SEE?

Look carefully at the picture.

You decide to go back to your trail and turn around to look for the way you came . . .

| A | B |

BUT...THIS IS WHAT YOU SEE BEHIND YOU.

CAN YOU REMEMBER THE WAY BACK?

First, find the buttress roots where you started on page 6. Remember, they are now behind the other plants you passed on the way. Then retrace your steps to the overhanging leaves.

| C | D |

THINK CAREFULLY . . .
IT'S **UP** TO **YOU** TO CHOOSE
WHICH DIRECTION IS THE WAY BACK.

A, B, C, or D?

You decide, then turn the page
to see if you are right.

ANSWERS

A. **WRONG.** After ten meters or so, you come across some broken-back twigs that look like they might be your path. You follow the trail as it winds in and out of the trees, until you come to a bare patch of mud where you find a track like this.
It's a tapir print!

6 inches

B. **WRONG.** Pushing through the undergrowth, you soon realize that nothing looks familiar. You decide to turn back, but which way is it?

C. **CORRECT.** Like a forest Indian, you have recognized the "landmarks," the leafy vines and the spiky stilt roots that show you how you got into this situation.

OVERHANGING LEAVES

TREE TRUNK WITH
THORNY ROOTS

TREE WITH
BUTTRESS ROOTS

D. **WRONG AGAIN, SUCKER.** All you find is a wasp nest and a type of ant with a particularly nasty bite.

See how easy it is to get lost?

Let's face it, the next step is to get **organized** and **equipped** – find out what to take to the rainforest and how to actually get there!

But first, before you set off,
here's a heroic story...

Isabella Godin
A JUNGLE SURVIVOR

1769: Frenchwoman Isabella Godin sets off from Quito (in what is now Ecuador) to cross the Amazon and meet up with her husband, Jean, who left France twenty years earlier. Traveling with her are her two brothers, a nephew, three maids, a slave called Joachim, and three other Frenchmen. They buy a large boat and hire around thirty Indians to paddle it for them.

Several days down river, the party arrives at a village where most of the population have died of smallpox. Petrified, the Indian paddlers flee into the jungle.

The group builds another canoe and finds a villager who has not died of smallpox to steer it for them. Unfortunately, the man is so ill that when the canoe capsizes, he drowns.

103

The three Frenchmen and Joachim take the canoe and set off downstream — they say — to get help. (Would you believe

Au Revoir! Back soon…promise!

them?) Isabella, her maids and relatives are left behind. They wait for twenty-five days, but no rescue arrives.

Sick and tired of all the waiting around, they build a raft out of balsa wood logs, but this falls apart when it hits a submerged tree trunk in the river. Isabella nearly drowns, but one of her brothers hauls her out of the water just in time. The group decides to set out on foot.

Soon they are lost, walking without food through track-less jungle. Everyone except Isabella dies. She stays with the bodies for two days, then sets off again, determined that she will survive. For nine days, she lives on what she can forage — just insects and roots. Her clothes are ripped to shreds by thorns and vines.

By the time she arrives at a river, her skin is a mass of bites and cuts, and her hair has gone white from all the stress. She must have been a pretty frightening sight to the two Indians who find her and take her to a missionary at their village.

In gratitude, Isabella breaks her gold necklace in half and gives the pieces to her rescuers. But the missionary takes the gold away from them and gives them cloth instead. Isabella is furious. She demands that the missionary give her a canoe and sets off down river, where she is soon rescued by a boat that has been hired by her father to find her. A Portuguese ship then takes her all the way down the Amazon and around the coast to where her husband is waiting to take her to France. He canoes out to meet the boat. It's been twenty years since they last set eyes on each other.

But, whatever happened to the other group? The three Frenchmen who had taken the canoe just took off — they never intended to go back for Isabella and the others. As for Joachim, he got to the missionary's village and took some Indians to search for the people left behind. He found the bodies and got back to the missionary's village shortly after Isabella had arrived. He was aboard the boat that picked her up.

About the author

Writer and broadcaster Simon Chapman is a self-confessed jungle addict, making expeditions whenever he can. His travels have taken him to tropical forests all over the world, from Borneo and Irian Jaya to the Amazon.

The story of his search for a mythical giant ape in the Bolivian rainforest, *The Monster of the Madidi*, was published in 2001. He has also had numerous articles and illustrations published in magazines in Britain and the United States, including *Wanderlust*, *BBC Wildlife*, and *South American Explorer*, and has written and recorded for BBC Radio 4, and lectured on the organization of jungle expeditions at the Royal Geographical Society, of which he is a fellow. When not exploring, Simon lives with his wife and his two young children in Lancaster, England, where he teaches high school physics.